BEGINNER WORD PROBLEMS

Minta Berry

Crabtree Publishing Company
www.crabtreebooks.com

Author: Minta Berry
Publishing plan research and development:
  Sean Charlebois, Reagan Miller
  Crabtree Publishing Company
Editor: Reagan Miller
Proofreader: Crystal Sikkens
Cover design: Margaret Amy Salter
Editorial director: Kathy Middleton
Production coordinator: Margaret Amy Salter
Prepress technician: Margaret Amy Salter
Print coordinator: Katherine Berti
Project manager: Kirsten Holm, Shivi Sharma
  (Planman Technologies)
Photo research: Iti Shrotriya (Planman Technologies)
Technical art: Arka Roy Chaudhary (Planman Technologies)

Photographs:
Cover: Gelpi/Shutterstock (girl), Margaret Amy Salter (butterflies);
(boundary) Lorelyn Medina/Shutterstock; P7: Kali Nine
LLC/IStockPhoto; P9: Michael C. Gray/Shutterstock; P11: (t) Elena
Blokhina/Shutterstock; (b) Dmitry Kalinovsky/Shutterstock; P13:
(t.bkgd.kitchen) ChandlerPhoto/IStockPhoto, (t.fgd.r) Kai
Wong/Shutterstock, (t.fgd.l) Yasonya/Shutterstock; (b) Jolanta
Mazus | Dreamstime.com; P 15: Alxpin/IStockPhoto; P17:
(boundary) Lorelyn Medina/Shutterstock; P21: (boundary)
Lorelyn Medina/Shutterstock.
(t = top, b = bottom, l = left, c= center, r = right,
bkgd = background, fgd = foreground)

Library and Archives Canada Cataloguing in Publication

Berry, Minta
    Beginner word problems / Minta Berry.

(My path to math)
Includes index.
Issued also in electronic formats.
ISBN 978-0-7787-5274-5 (bound).--ISBN 978-0-7787-5263-9 (pbk.)

    1. Word problems (Mathematics)--Juvenile literature. 2. Problem
solving--Juvenile literature. I. Title. II. Series: My path to math.

QA63.B465 2011   j510   C2011-906798-6

Library of Congress Cataloging-in-Publication Data

Berry, Minta.
  Beginner word problems / Minta Berry.
      p. cm. -- (My path to math)
  Includes index.
  ISBN 978-0-7787-5274-5 (reinforced library binding : alk. paper) -- ISBN 978-
0-7787-5263-9 (pbk. : alk. paper) -- ISBN 978-1-4271-8804-5 (electronic pdf) --
ISBN 978-1-4271-9645-3 (electronic html)
  1. Word problems (Mathematics)--Juvenile literature. 2. Problem solving--
Juvenile literature. I. Title.
  QA63.B47 2012
  510--dc23
                                                        2011040400

Crabtree Publishing Company

Printed in the U.S.A./112011/JA20111018

www.crabtreebooks.com   1-800-387-7650

Published in Canada
Crabtree Publishing
616 Welland Ave.
St. Catharines, ON
L2M 5V6

Published in the United States
Crabtree Publishing
PMB 59051
350 Fifth Avenue, 59th Floor
New York, New York 10118

Published in the United Kingdom
Crabtree Publishing
Maritime House
Basin Road North, Hove
BN41 1WR

Published in Australia
Crabtree Publishing
3 Charles Street
Coburg North
VIC 3058

Contents

Steps to Solve Word Problems

Carmen and Aiden are learning how to solve **word problems**. They learn five important steps to solving word problems. Their teacher makes a poster listing the steps to hang in their classroom.

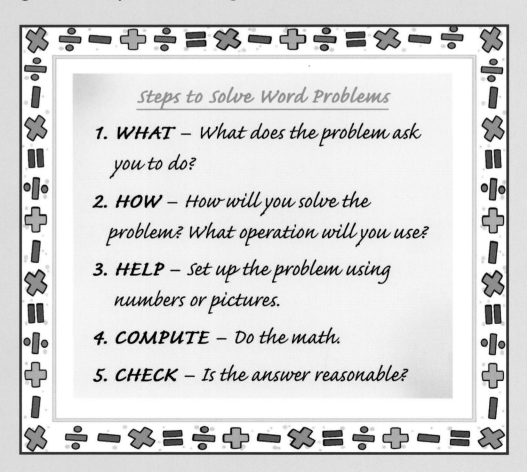

Steps to Solve Word Problems

1. **WHAT** – What does the problem ask you to do?

2. **HOW** – How will you solve the problem? What operation will you use?

3. **HELP** – Set up the problem using numbers or pictures.

4. **COMPUTE** – Do the math.

5. **CHECK** – Is the answer reasonable?

Word Problem # 1

Three frogs are sitting on a lily pad. Two more frogs jump onto the lily pad. How many frogs in total are sitting on the lily pad?

Carmen tells Aiden that she looks for word clues to help her solve math problems. Carmen explains that the words "in total" are a clue that tells her she needs to add to solve the math problem.

Carmen draws a picture to help solve the problem.

Aiden looks at her answer. He knows that three plus two is five. He tells Carmen that her answer looks right.

Activity Box

Six fish are in a fish tank. Amit puts three more fish in the tank. How many fish are in the tank altogether?

Use the five steps to solve the word problem.

?

State the Problem

Aiden's teacher says it helps to repeat a word problem in your own words.

Aiden reads the problem. Then he repeats the word problem using his own words. "I need to find out how many students there are. Some students are fishing. Some are rock climbing. I will add them to find the total."

The teacher was right! Using his own words helps Aiden understand the problem.

> **Word Problem # 2**
>
> Students choose to fish or rock climb. There are 10 students fishing. Four students are rock climbing. How many students are there altogether?

Steps to Solve Word Problems
1. **WHAT** – What does the problem ask you to do?
2. **HOW** – How will you solve the problem? What operation will you use?
3. **HELP** – Set up the problem using numbers or pictures.
4. **COMPUTE** – Do the math.
5. **CHECK** – Is the answer reasonable?

Aiden and Carmen read their word problems to each other.

Tips for Stating Problems in Your Own Words

- Read the word problem. Put it in your own words. Then read the word problem again.

- Write your own words using short sentences.

- Use simple words.

- Write number words as symbols.

- State the operation you will use.

- Read your word problem to a friend. Use their ideas to improve your problem.

Activity Box

There are eight wooden buildings in the pioneer village. Two of the buildings are on this side of the creek. The rest are on the other side. How many buildings are on the other side?

Read the two statements of the problem.
Which statement is correct?

I need to find out how many buildings there are in total. I can add the 8 buildings to the 2 buildings on this side of the creek.

I need to find how many buildings are across the creek. There are 8 buildings altogether. I need to subtract the two on this side of the creek. That will tell me how many buildings are on the other side.

Operation Words

Carmen and Aiden use two **operations** to solve their word problems. They use **addition** and **subtraction**.

Many word problems are **one-step word problems**. You use one operation to solve the problem.

Word problems do not tell you which operation to use. But they do include clues in the words they use.

Operation Clue Words

Addition +	Subtraction −
altogether	how much more
in all	how much taller
in total	change
sum	how many less
total cost	how many more
	difference
	minus
	how much left

Word Problem #3

Aiden and his dad are going to the movies. Aiden wants to treat his dad to popcorn. He has $3. The popcorn is $5. How much more money does Aiden need?

In this word problem, the words "how much more" gives Aiden a clue. He needs to use subtraction to solve the problem.

$$\$5.00 - \$3.00 = \$2.00$$

Aiden needs $2.00 more to buy the popcorn.

Steps to Solve Word Problems

1. **WHAT** – What does the problem ask you to do?
2. **HOW** – How will you solve the problem? What operation will you use?
3. **HELP** – Set up the problem using numbers or pictures.
4. **COMPUTE** – Do the math.
5. **CHECK** – Is the answer reasonable?

Activity Box

One week Carmen gives her dog five treats. The next week she gives him eight treats. How many dog treats has Carmen given her dog in all?

Read the word problem. What words tell you the operation to use? What operation should you use? Draw a picture to help you solve the problem.

?

Does Your Answer Make Sense?

Carmen reads the word problem. She states it in her own words. Then she figures out which operation to use. Next, she writes a **number sentence** to solve the problem.

Aiden also writes a number sentence to solve the problem.

> ### Word Problem # 4
>
> Daniel walks up the stairs in his apartment building. He starts on the third floor. He walks up to the ninth floor. This is the top floor in the building. How many floors has he climbed?

Aiden's Number Sentence	**Carmen's Number Sentence**
3 + 9 = 12	9 – 3 = 6

Carmen checks if her answer makes sense.

Carmen sees that the ninth floor is the top floor. She knows that the answer must be less than nine. Carmen says that her answer is more **reasonable**. Aiden agrees.

Steps to Solve Word Problems

1. **WHAT** – What does the problem ask you to do?
2. **HOW** – How will you solve the problem? What operation will you use?
3. **HELP** – Set up the problem using numbers or pictures.
4. **COMPUTE** – Do the math.
5. **CHECK** – Is the answer reasonable?

Activity Box

The petting zoo has nine chicks and five rabbits. How many more chicks than rabbits are there?

Number Sentence 1	**Number Sentence 2**
9 – 5 = 4	9 + 5 = 14

Read the word problem. Which answer is reasonable? Why?

Find Unimportant Information

Sometimes word problems have extra details or information that do not help solve the problem. Skip this information when stating the problem in your own words.

What information is not needed? Aiden does not need to know whether a tomato is a fruit or a vegetable. He leaves this information out of his problem statement.

Word Problem # 5

The tomato is a fruit, although some people think it is a vegetable. Sara picked 3 tomatoes from one plant on Tuesday. She picked 10 tomatoes from another plant on Friday. How many more tomatoes did she pick on Friday than she picked on Tuesday?

In Aiden's Words

"Sara picked 3 tomatoes on Tuesday. She picked 10 tomatoes on Friday. I need to subtract to find how many more tomatoes she picked on Friday.

10 tomatoes – 3 tomatoes = 7 tomatoes

Aiden reads the problem again. His answer makes sense. He knows that Sara picked more tomatoes on Friday than on Tuesday.

Activity Box

Daesha visits the snake house at the zoo. One snake is seven feet long. The other snake is five feet long. If they stretched out nose to nose, how long are the snakes altogether?

What information in the word problem is not needed? Follow the steps to solve the word problem.

Write and Illustrate Your Own Problem

Aiden wants to be a race car driver. Carmen gives Aiden a number sentence. She tells him to use her number sentence to write his own word problem about car racing.

16 + 3 = 19

Aiden's Word Problem

The crowd was on their feet, cheering as I sped around the track. I drove 16 laps in record time. After three more laps I will become world champion! How many laps will I race in total?

Carmen reads Aiden's word problem. She writes the problem in her own words. She remembers to leave out unimportant information that will not help solve the problem.

$$
\begin{array}{r}
16 \text{ laps} \\
+\ 3 \text{ laps} \\
\hline
19 \text{ laps}
\end{array}
$$

In Carmen's Words

"Aiden drove 16 laps. Then he drove 3 laps. I need to add to find the total."

Activity Box

18 − 2 = 16

Use the number sentence above to write your own word problem. Include some unimportant information. Remember to use clue words. Also, draw a picture to show your problem.

Solve Two-Step Word Problems

Some word problems use more than one operation. They are called **two-step word problems**. Find the clue words in the problem. The first clue word usually tells you which operation to do first.

Write the problem in your own words. Figure out which operation to do first. Then write which operation comes second.

Aiden reads the problem, then writes it in his own words.

> ### Word Problem # 6
>
> A class travels around the museum village in a train. The train had 12 people on it already. The class adds 18 students. The train seats 36 people. How many seats are left after all the students get on the train?

Step 1 is addition.

Step 2 is subtraction.

$$\begin{array}{r} {}^1 12 \\ +18 \\ \hline 30 \end{array}$$

$$\begin{array}{r} 36 \\ -30 \\ \hline 6 \end{array}$$

In Aiden's Words

"There are 12 people on a train. Then 18 students get on the train. I need to add to find the total number of people. The train seats 36. I subtract the total number of people from 36."

Steps to Solve Two-Step Word Problems

1. **WHAT** – What does the problem ask you to do?

2. **HOW** – How will you solve the problem? **What operation will you use first?**

3. **HELP** – Set up the problem using numbers or pictures.

4. **COMPUTE** – Do the operations in the correct order.

5. **CHECK** – Is the answer reasonable?

The teacher makes a new poster. It shows the steps to solve two-step word problems.

Tips for Two-Step Problems

✔ Look for clue words.

✔ The problem usually tells about the operations in order.

✔ State the problem in your own words. Then read the problem again. Make sure all facts are stated.

✔ Think about what the problem is asking.

✔ If a word problem asks more than one question, answer both.

Activity Box

Carmen wants to buy a $3.00 stuffed dinosaur and a $9.00 book about spiders. She has $15.00. Does she have enough money to buy both items?

Follow the steps to solve this two-step word problem.

Use Models to Solve Word Problems

A **model** is a picture, graph, or chart. Models help to see how to solve a problem. The teacher gives Carmen and Aiden a graph showing book sales at the school book fair. She also gives them a two-step word problem.

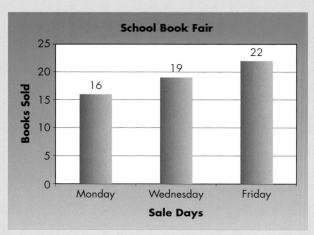

Aiden uses all the steps to solve the problem.

Step 1 is addition.

$$\begin{array}{r} \overset{1}{1}6 \\ 19 \\ +22 \\ \hline 57 \end{array}$$

Step 2 is subtraction.

$$\begin{array}{r} \overset{1}{\cancel{2}}\overset{1}{2} \\ -16 \\ \hline 6 \end{array}$$

Word Problem # 7

Use the graph to answer these questions. How many books were sold altogether? How many more books were sold on Friday than on Monday?

The total number of books sold is 57. The difference between sales on Friday and Monday is 6 books.

Word Problem # 8

The people at the museum give stickers to the children. The children answer questions to earn the stickers. Andrea gets six stickers. Mackenzie gets four stickers. Zach gets two more stickers than Andrea. How many stickers does Zach get? How many total stickers do the three students get altogether?

Carmen makes a chart to help her solve the problem.

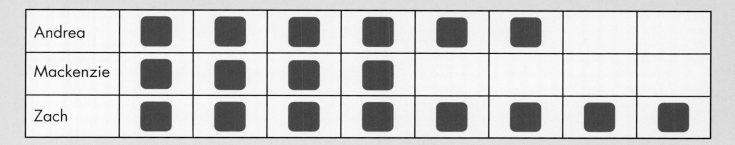

Zach gets 8 stickers. The students get a total of 6 + 4 + 8 = 18 stickers.

Activity Box

Use the graph to solve the word problem. A museum invites school groups to visit. What is the total number of visits over the three years? What is the difference between the first year and the third year?

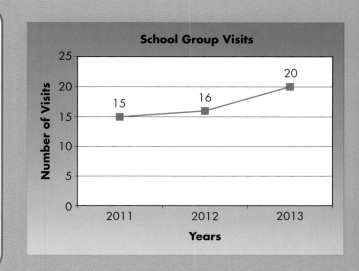

Follow the steps to solve this two-step word problem.

Write a Two-Step Word Problem

The teacher gives Carmen and Aiden two number sentences. They use the sentences to write their own two-step word problem.

3 + 5 + 2 = 10
10 – 5 = 5

Carmen writes a word problem about her friends. Aiden reads the problem. He follows the steps to solve Carmen's two-step problem.

Carmen's Word Problem

Brandon, Tonya, and I go to the playground. We find five friends waiting for us. Then Amy and Bobby come. We play for 20 minutes. Then five friends leave. The rest play until dark. How many friends played together that day in all? How many play until dark?

In Aiden's Words

"Carmen and her 2 friends go to the playground. They meet 5 friends. Then 2 more friends come. I need to add to find the total. Then I subtract the 5 people who left. This leaves the number of friends who stayed."

20   3 + 5 + 2 = 10 friends   10 – 5 = 5 friends remain

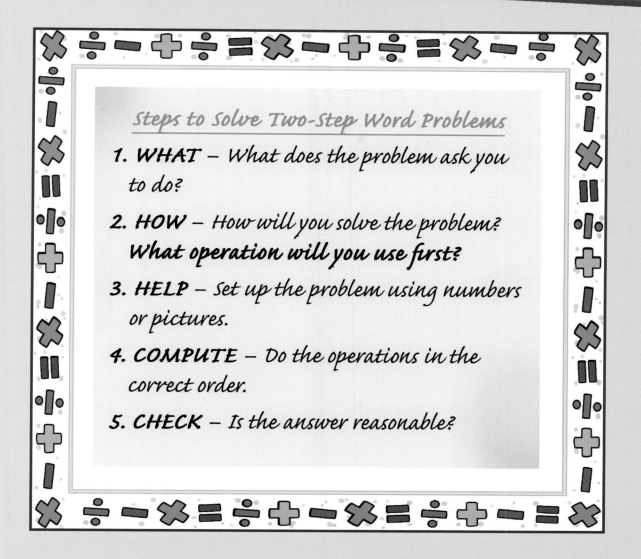

Steps to Solve Two-Step Word Problems

1. **WHAT** – What does the problem ask you to do?

2. **HOW** – How will you solve the problem? **What operation will you use first?**

3. **HELP** – Set up the problem using numbers or pictures.

4. **COMPUTE** – Do the operations in the correct order.

5. **CHECK** – Is the answer reasonable?

Copy these problem-solving steps to create your own poster. Hang it in an area where you do your math homework.

Activity Box

9 + 4 = 13

13 – 6 = 7

Use the number sentences above to write a two-step word problem. Remember to use clue words. Include a model if you can.

Glossary

addition Finding the total or sum by combining two or more numbers

model A picture, graph, or chart that gives math facts or helps to solve a math problem

number sentence A math sentence using numbers (1, 2, 3) and symbols (+, =)

one-step word problem One operation is needed to solve the problem

operations Math process such as addition or subtraction

reasonable Something that makes sense

subtraction Taking one number away from another number

two-step word problem A word problem that uses two operations

word problems Math problems written in sentences

Steps to Solve One-Step Word Problems

1. **WHAT** – What does the problem ask you to do?
2. **HOW** – How will you solve the problem?
   What operation will you use?
3. **HELP** – Set up the problem using numbers or pictures.
4. **COMPUTE** – Do the math.
5. **CHECK** – Is the answer reasonable?

Steps to Solve Two-Step Word Problems

1. **WHAT** – What does the problem ask you to do?
2. **HOW** – How will you solve the problem?
   What operation will you use first?
3. **HELP** – Set up the problem using numbers or pictures.
4. **COMPUTE** – Do the operations in the correct order.
5. **CHECK** – Is the answer reasonable?

Index